HEADLINE SERIES

No. 313   FOREIGN POLICY ASSOCIATION   Winter

Does Russia Have A Democratic Future?

by Allen C. Lynch

Introduction 3

1 The Soviet Legacy
   for Post-Communist Russia 10

2 Russia's Political Institutions 17

3 The Crisis of the Russian State 36

4 Does Russia Have
   a Democratic Future? 50

5 Implications for American
   Foreign Policy 61

   Talking It Over 69

   Annotated Reading List 70

Cover Design: Ed Bohon $5.95

The Author

ALLEN C. LYNCH, director of the Center for Russian and East European Studies and associate professor of government and foreign affairs at the University of Virginia, received a Ph.D. in political science from Columbia University. From 1989 to 1992, he was assistant director of the W. Averell Harriman Institute for Advanced Study of the Soviet Union at Columbia. A specialist in Russian foreign policy and East-West relations, he is the author of many books and articles.

For Mom, Dad, and Mamma

The Foreign Policy Association

The Foreign Policy Association is a private, nonprofit, nonpartisan educational organization. Its purpose is to stimulate wider interest and more effective participation in, and greater understanding of, world affairs among American citizens. Among its activities is the continuous publication, dating from 1935, of the HEADLINE SERIES. The author is responsible for factual accuracy and for the views expressed. FPA itself takes no position on issues of U.S. foreign policy.

HEADLINE SERIES (ISSN 0017-8780) is published four times a year, Spring, Summer, Fall and Winter, by the Foreign Policy Association, Inc., 470 Park Avenue So., New York, NY 10016. Chairman, Paul B. Ford; President, Noel V. Lateef; Editor in Chief, Nancy Hoepli-Phalon; Senior Editors, Ann R. Monjo and K.M. Rohan; Assistant Editor, Nicholas Barratt. Subscription rates, $20.00 for 4 issues; $35.00 for 8 issues; $50.00 for 12 issues. Single copy price $5.95; double issue $11.25. Discount 25% on 10 to 99 copies; 30% on 100 to 499; 35% on 500 and over. Payment must accompany all orders. Postage and handling, $2.50 for first copy; $.50 each additional copy. Second-class postage paid at New York, NY, and additional mailing offices. POSTMASTER: Send address changes to HEADLINE SERIES, Foreign Policy Association, 470 Park Avenue So., New York, NY 10016. Copyright 1997 by Foreign Policy Association, Inc. Design by K.M. Rohan. Printed at Science Press, Ephrata, Pennsylvania. Winter 1995. Published September 1997.

Library of Congress Catalog Card No. 97-60997
ISBN 0-87124-177-3

Introduction

A form of government that is not the result of a long sequence of shared experiences, efforts and endeavors can never take root.

—Napoleon Bonaparte, 1803

IT WAS THE FIRST of the two Russian revolutions of 1917 that gave substance to President Woodrow Wilson's call for the United States to "make the world safe for democracy" through its intervention in World War I. The sudden collapse of the czarist monarchy and the establishment of a liberal democratic Russian government under the leadership of Aleksandr F. Kerensky in the winter of 1917 gave credence to the hopes of American democrats that an Allied military victory over Imperial Germany would usher in an age of universal democracy and with it universal peace. The tide of democratic sentiment also flowed westward from the Russian capital of Petrograd (St. Petersburg), where Kerensky's government, anxious to convince its British, French and now American allies of Russia's

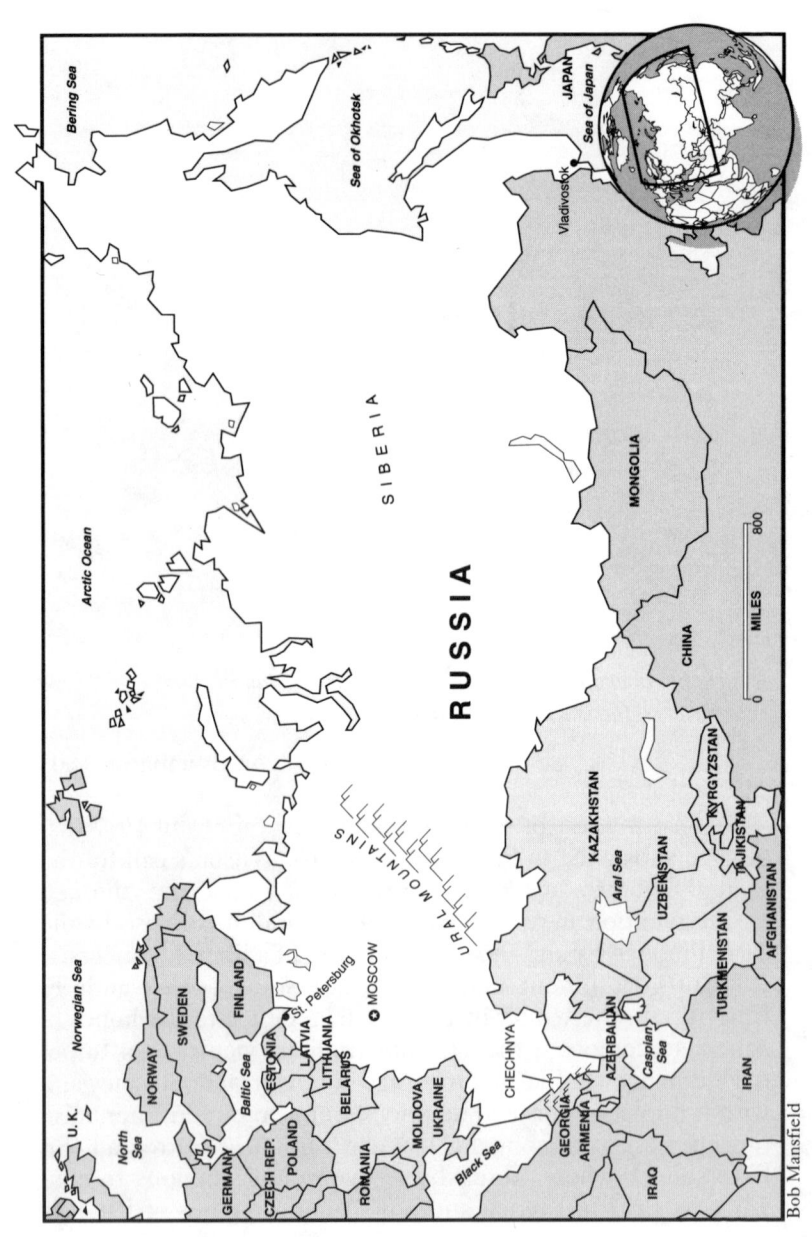

newfound democratic allegiance, kept a grieviously weakened Russia engaged in a third full year of war with Germany and launched ill-conceived offensives that, by the summer of 1917, had resulted in the disintegration of the Russian army as an effective combat force. Sir George Buchanan, the British ambassador in Petrograd, wondered to his diary whether the Western democracies might better have set aside the military pledges they had extracted from what had become a gravely weak Russia and let the country negotiate its own path out of the war. In the end, the continuation of Russia's involvement in the "war for democracy" proved to be perhaps the decisive trigger for the second Russian revolution of 1917 and the establishment of a Communist regime that autumn.

The sudden disintegration of President Mikhail S. Gorbachev's Soviet Union in December 1991 and the emergence of an independent Russian Federation under its president, Boris N. Yeltsin, that was openly committed to the ideals and institutions of Western democracy, took up the promise that the first revolution in February 1917 appeared to hold out. Political democracy, and with it the establishment of an economy along Western capitalist lines, is the avowed aim of Russia's post-Soviet government. Russia's government, moreover, has been seeking a broad diplomatic and economic partnership with the advanced industrial democracies, including, where possible, integration into Western political, economic and even security institutions. The policies of many governments, including those of the United States, have been aimed at bolstering what they see as the "reform" government of Russian President Yeltsin: by cementing Russia's democratic and capitalist foundations, they believe they are laying the groundwork for a stable and reasonably harmonious relationship between Russia and the advanced capitalist democracies. Then Secretary of State Warren Christopher summarized the U.S. view in March 1995 by noting, "The successful transformation of the former Soviet Union into a region of sovereign, democratic states is a matter of fundamental importance to the United States."

The purpose of this book is to examine the premises of this approach to post-Soviet Russia. What *are* Russia's democratic prospects? How do Russia's post-Soviet institutions and the state of Russian opinion—elite and mass—encourage or retard the development of a democratic political system? To what extent does the rise of new kinds of post-Soviet criminal networks both reflect and affect Russia's post-Communist political system? What is the relationship between Russia's political system and the kind of foreign policy that the Russian government has been and is likely to continue pursuing? Finally, what are the implications of Russia's democratic prospects for U.S. foreign policy and relations between the two countries?

The Prerequisites of Democracy

All contemporary stable democratic political systems rest on a capitalist economic foundation. Moreover, a functioning rule of law is required for the holders of capital to assess the risks that necessarily follow investment in an economy's future. Not all capitalist economies sustain political democracies, however, and in this respect capitalism may be considered a necessary but not sufficient precondition for the establishment of political democracy. Indeed, the question of institutions is only one part of the democratic equation. The other concerns what might be called the democratic spirit— the basic attitudes, values and concept of humanity and its place in society. Political theorist Hans Kohn has made the following distinctions between the attitudes, method and institutions of democracy: In terms of fundamental attitudes and values, democracy "presupposes the existence of opposition as a legitimate partner in the democratic process; it accepts a pluralistic view of values and associations, and it rejects any totalitarian or monolithic identification of the state with one party or with one dogma." Considered as a way of life, democracy reflects that "attitude by which the members of the community are led to secure to every one his rights, to look upon all fellow citizens without distinction of color or race as brethren in a common enterprise, and to give spontaneous support to projects which

Reuters/Natruskin/Archive Photos

Russian President Boris Yeltsin with his daughter Tatyana, who is now an official adviser. They are shown strolling in Yekaterinburg with a city official during an election trip in July 1996.

enhance civic excellence and promote the general welfare." In this respect, then, tolerance and civic-mindedness are core components of democracy.

Kohn defined the "method of democracy" as "the method of discussion, of open-minded critical inquiry, and finally and frequently of compromise." Yet it is also true that critical inquiry and even compromise, as well as tolerance and civic-mindedness, are compatible with nondemocratic political systems, such as the benevolent despotism that the Greek philosopher Aristotle considered the ideal form of polity. But since none can predict when the admittedly rare enlightened despot will emerge, or, rarer still, that his or her power will be bequeathed to an equally enlightened successor, democratic values and methods require certain types of institutions to survive and flourish. At heart, as Harvard University's Samuel

Huntington has observed in his award-winning 1991 book, *The Third Wave: Democratization in the Late Twentieth Century*, democracy requires institutions that allow effective choice over who shall rule and meaningful participation in the process of government. If, as Kohn wrote, political democracy is conceived as a form of government "based upon self-rule of the people and in modern times upon freely elected representative institutions and an executive responsible to the people," then a number of institutions are necessary for democratic values to express themselves. These include:

(1) a popular constitution, which expresses the consent by which the people establish the state; creates a specific form of government; and both grants and limits the powers which the government is to possess;

(2) a system of representative government, based on a parliament that is chosen through elections run on the principle of universal suffrage; and

(3) a relatively disciplined system of political parties that connects popular opinion to the governmental process and frames meaningful public debate and legislation on issues of civic importance.

A key *social* precondition for stable political democracy is the existence of a relatively large, prosperous, well-educated and secure middle class—or at least one which, if small, is growing rather than contracting—which believes that its interests and values are and will continue to be protected by the democratic process. In this respect, a degree of economic well-being and socioeconomic equality are critical to the democratic enterprise.

To summarize, then, political democracy has a political-institutional foundation in the agencies and procedures of representative government; a social-psychological foundation in the prevalence of toleration and civic spirit in the citizenry; and a social-economic foundation in economic well-being and a relatively large and secure middle class.

By these standards, it is most unlikely that Russia can in any policy-relevant future become a liberal, market democracy. Too many preconditions for market democracy are absent: the rule of law, a stable middle class, a broad commitment to individualism, compromise and trust in civic affairs. At best, Russia's foreseeable political stability will be highly fragile, due precisely to the effort to construct simultaneously a political democracy and a capitalist economy in the absence of reasonably competent institutions of governance. As a result, Russia's primary political challenge is not so much the construction of a liberal democracy as it is the establishment of a minimally competent state, a cruel irony in light of Russia's historical challenge of taming overweening state authority. Yet the debility of Russia's post-Soviet public institutions means that for Russia even to have a chance at the development of the rule of law, not to mention political democracy, the establishment of such a state is as important as the emergence of a vital and democratically committed civil society.

1

The Soviet Legacy for Post-Communist Russia

WESTERN Sovietologists have been broadly, if perhaps unfairly, criticized for not anticipating the rapid (and relatively peaceful) collapse of the Soviet Union in late 1991. Yet the same may be said of Soviet and Russian politicians themselves: until practically the last minute in December 1991, nearly all nationalist leaders in Russia, Ukraine, Belarus, as well as in the Central Asian republics of the Soviet Union, expected a prolonged transitional period in which power would gradually devolve to the constituent national republics through negotiation with the Soviet central government. They did not expect, and were consequently almost completely unprepared for, the rapid disappearance of the Soviet state and thus for the assumption of the responsibilities of governing fully independent states.

This unpreparedness was compounded by the fact that the sudden disintegration of the Soviet system, based as it was on the virtual monopoly of all public organizations by an integrated Communist party-state system of rule, left the Soviet successor

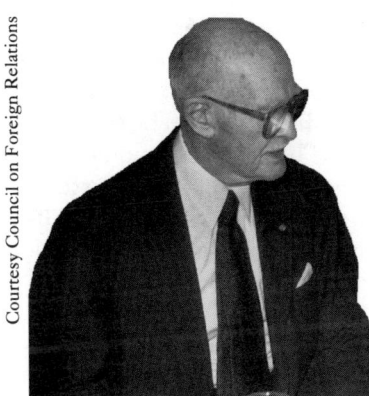

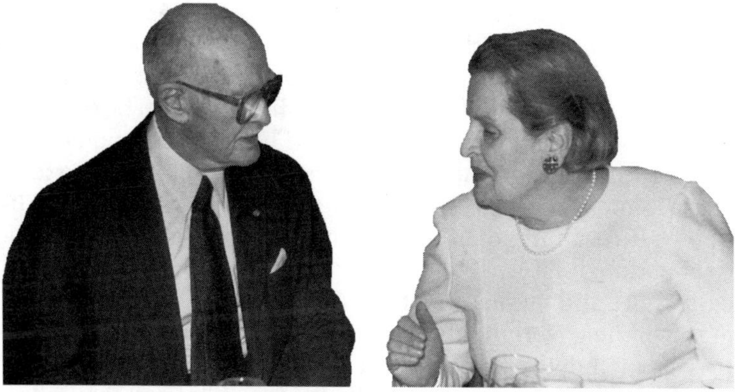
Courtesy Council on Foreign Relations

George F. Kennan, former diplomat and educator who has influenced U.S. policy toward Russia for a half century, at Council on Foreign Relations dinner in honor of his 90th birthday in 1994 with now Secretary of State Madeleine K. Albright.

states as a rule with few of the institutions required to chart a stable post-Soviet political course, democratic or otherwise. One of the few observers to contemplate the political dynamics that could lead to the kind of collapse that occurred in 1991 was the U.S. diplomat George F. Kennan, who speculated in 1947 in *Foreign Affairs* magazine on what might happen if a successor to Soviet leader Joseph Stalin should ever attempt to mobilize constituents outside of the Communist party elite in the quest for higher power:

> *If disunity were ever to seize and paralyze the party, the chaos and weakness of Russian society would be revealed in forms beyond description....Soviet power is only a crust concealing an amorphous mass of human beings among whom no independent organizational structure is tolerated. In Russia there is not even such a thing as local government. The present generation of Russians have never known spontaneity of collective action. If, consequently, anything were ever done to disrupt the unity and efficacy of the party as a political instrument, Soviet Russia might be changed overnight from one of the strongest to one of the weakest and most pitiable of national societies.*

Four decades would pass before Kennan's prophecy took hold. Only in the Gorbachev period (1985–91) would the Soviet government, reflecting Gorbachev's control of the party-state apparatus, push economic and political reform beyond the party's structural limits of tolerance. The disintegration of the U.S.S.R. ended not only a particular kind of political system, i.e., the totalitarian party-state, but also a centuries-old tradition of Russian imperial rule, as the U.S.S.R. split into 15 distinct national states. The legacy of the Russian/Soviet imperial party-state and the nature of its collapse frame the choices facing all of the governments and peoples in the post-Soviet states, Russia included. As Columbia University political scientist Alexander J. Motyl has noted, all of these states are compelled by force of circumstances to face two enormous political challenges: first, to build effective political, economic and legal institutions practically from the ground up in the wake of the collapse of the Soviet economy and state; second, and even more difficult, to build all of these institutions at the same time. Consider only that the construction of certain kinds of institutions is a precondition of the effectiveness of others, and the instabilities of post-Soviet political-economic development become apparent. That is, while "democracy" may be the ultimate aim (for many, it clearly is not), an effectively functioning market economy appears to be a historically demonstrated prerequisite for political democracy itself. Likewise, it is hard to see how a modern market economy can be established without an effectively functioning legal system, which is itself predicated upon the existence of a strong and competent state and state administration. In the final analysis, strong democracies are also strong (that is, competent) states.

The Missing Foundations

It is difficult to see how, given the post-Soviet lack of effective public institutions, a rapid and stable progression from formerly totalitarian and imperial to recognizably pluralist political systems can be made. Without a state that is able to perform the minimum functions of governance (raising sufficient taxes, controlling the military, enforcing the law), the legal and economic foundations for constitutional government, not to speak of democracy, cannot be laid. Unfortunately, many of the voices calling for a strong state are also those most opposed to democracy, a market economy and the rule of law.

Moreover, the simultaneous introduction of market economics and electoral democracy means that the broad swaths of Russian society that are being economically and socially disenfranchised are also being enfranchised politically. In this context, one of two outcomes is likely: either the economically and socially disenfranchised majority will express their interest in maximum social security through the ballot and elect representatives far less favorable to market economics than the Russian government has recently been, or the new economic and social elites will seek to protect their gains by direct and indirect subversion of the democratic process. The best-case scenario—the rapid and *stable* transformation of the Russian Federation into a functioning democracy and mature market economy—is thus implausible.

Equally implausible is what many Americans imagine to be the worst-case scenario. The collapse of the Soviet political economy means that there is simply no way back to the Soviet past, in terms of a party-state monopoly of the political and economic systems or the revival of a challenge for global or even Eurasian hegemony. Yet absent these two extreme possibilities, almost all of the futures that one could imagine for Russia are plausible.

In many respects, post-Soviet Russia remains faced with the same problem that bedeviled Gorbachev: How to maintain the integrity of what remains in Russia a federal, multinational state while at the same time reorganizing the distribution of power within that state so as to modernize politically, economically and socially? The course of Russian politics through the first years of independence was far from encouraging in this respect: 1992 and 1993 were plagued by perpetual political warfare between the executive and legislative branches of government, culminating in the bloody suppression of the Russian parliament by Russian army tanks on October 4, 1993. Not only were the president and the legislature pursuing mutually exclusive policies—focused on the scope and pace of price liberalization and the privatization of industry—but they were each claiming mutually exclusive jurisdiction within the political system. Furthermore, there were no generally accepted constitutional procedures (such as a vote of confidence) for resolving such a governmental impasse. The explosive culmination of the Russian political stalemate in the streets of Moscow in early October 1993 thus represented the functional (if violent) equivalent of a vote of confidence, in that it "resolved" the crisis of power in favor of the Russian president, who assumed classically dictatorial powers pending parliamentary elections in December 1993 (which, in fact, proved to be a decisive defeat for Yeltsin's political supporters).

If 1993 saw the emergence of a new political order in Russia, 1994 saw that order put to significant tests. Throughout 1994 and frequently since, many Russian and outside observers have remarked on the puzzling stability that has seemed to prevail in politics and society. The comprehensive disintegration of the previous, Soviet-era institutions of public authority, the continued collapse of the industrial economy, and a growing polarization in the society as well as in the polity, did not lead to the sorts of political confrontations typical of 1992 and 1993, which had seemed destined to become endemic to post-Soviet Russian politics. Had Yeltsin's Russia reached some sort of precarious equilibrium, one that eluded Gorbachev as well as Yeltsin himself in his first two years as president of the independent Russian Federation?

Before 1994 was out, a series of events, most prominently the Russian invasion of Chechnya, suggested that post-Soviet Russia was failing the most fundamental tests of political stability. The calamity of the Russian government's invasion of the secessionist province of Chechnya in December 1994 underscored in the most dramatic fashion the failure of Yeltsin's government to impart the minimum of institutional coherence to the activities and functioning of government in post-Communist Russia.

The decision by a handful of Yeltsin's security ministers to invade showed just how weak Russia's parliament and civil society were; the defeat eventually suffered by the Russian armed forces in failing to suppress the Chechen rebellion showed just how weak the Russian state had become.

Whether one speaks of the fate of economic reform (including the vaunted "success" of privatization and the limited capacity of the central government to levy taxes), the collapse of civilian control over the military, as well as the frequent collapse of the military's control over its own subordinate units, or the disintegration of the Russian army as a coherent combat organization, the preconditions for minimally effective government in Russia (not to mention a government committed to

Reuters/Volodva Svartsevich/Archive Photos

August 1996: In Grozny, Chechnya, 20 months after Russian troops invaded the secessionist province in a failed attempt to subdue it, rebel fighters ride a captured Russian tank through ruins.

economic or political reform) have been seriously challenged. The Russian state is unable to shape effectively most of its economic, social and political environment. Russia has appeared stable since late 1993 because those with the power to destabilize Russia—i.e., the numerous alliances throughout Russia of the former Communist industrial elite, military and police units, and openly criminal elements—have been essentially satisfied with a weak state. Russian "stability" could be preserved as long as the state did not attempt a display of force, one that, as Chechnya shows, was likely to fail and which would make explicit the reality that the Russian government is little able to reward its friends or punish its foes. Not only has the war in Chechnya displayed the profound weakness of Russia's political and military institutions, but the political and economic costs of the war weigh heavily on already fragile Russian political and economic systems.

Finally, there is a fateful irony in the legacy of Soviet collapse. Many in the old Soviet elite were able to exploit the administrative chaos of Gorbachev's last years in power to control the privatization of much of Soviet state property, which included nearly the entire industrial economy. In effect, Soviet bureaucrats quickly figured out how to convert their administrative control of state assets into their personal private property, thereby insulating themselves from the consequences of the disintegration of the Communist system and the Soviet state. The fact that the U.S.S.R. fell apart as peacefully as it did, avoiding the generalized violence that beset Yugoslavia, is no doubt related to the belief among many in the Soviet elite that they had thereby found a way to escape the personal consequences of the Soviet collapse. Yet this triumph of private over public considerations, which helped the Russian people to avoid the worst, also constrains Russia's political and economic prospects. Russia's "new" political-economic elites have proved either incapable or unwilling to assert the primacy of the public good over the private interest in order to shepherd the Russian nation through its painful post-Soviet transition.

2

Russia's Political Institutions

AT FIRST GLANCE, post-Soviet Russia possesses all of the institutions characteristic of political democracies: a written constitution approved by popular vote; a bicameral representative parliament selected on the basis of universal suffrage; multiple political parties broadly reflecting the range of opinion in the country; an executive presidency accountable to the people through direct elections; as well as a multitude of newspapers expressing often highly critical views of government policy. What is the nature of Russia's political institutions and how do they work in actual practice? In particular, what does the functioning of Russia's institutions imply about Russia's democratic prospects?

The Constitution

Russia's written constitution, adopted in December 1993 after a nationwide referendum, is a direct product of the struggles between parliament and president in 1992 and 1993 over the ultimate source of power. These struggles, which were intensified by the absence of a mechanism such as a vote of confidence in the Soviet-based constitution of the time, were ultimately resolved by bullet instead of ballot. Armored units of the Russian army, at President Yeltsin's orders, shelled the Russian parliament building and forced the surrender of the coalition of Communists and extreme nationalists which had defied Yeltsin's authority and had themselves begun to resort to force of arms to press their cause. Yeltsin, who had, by his own admission, unconstitutionally suspended the parliament in September 1993, sought to justify his actions by calling for early parliamentary elections and a referendum on a new constitution. Those elections of December 1993 resulted in a crushing defeat for the Russian president's allies and brought to parliament a majority not very different from the coalition that Yeltsin had physically destroyed just two months earlier. At the same time, in a procedure that remains controversial to this day, Yeltsin's government claimed a majority vote for a constitution that established a superpresidentialist form of government, thereby ratifying in constitutional terms Yeltsin's recent military victory over his political opponents.

Parliament Subservient to President

Drawing from aspects of the U.S. and French presidential systems, the post-1993 Russian constitution firmly establishes the supremacy of president over parliament, even if certain checks and balances are formally included. For example, whereas previously a simple majority in parliament could override a presidential decision, now a two-thirds vote of both the State Duma (parliament), representing the population as a whole, and the Council of the Federation, representing Russia's federal units, is required. Whereas before, the president and parliament contested the authority to appoint the government, the new constitution gives this power to the president. While the parliament may reject the president's choice for prime minister, should it do so three times, the president may dissolve the parliament and call for new elections. Similarly, the parliament may vote no confidence in the government, but the president may ignore the first such vote. If the vote is repeated within three months, the president is obligated to respond, but he may choose to dismiss the parliament instead of the government. Moreover, the president may simply dismiss the government without taking into account the views of the parliament. The president is also granted the power to declare a state of emergency and govern (temporarily) by unfettered presidential *diktat*. The budget is determined by the presidentially appointed government, not the parliament, although the latter must approve the state budget. It must also be recalled that any temptation that parliament may have to confront the president is undoubtedly tempered by the precedents that President Yeltsin has set for employing military force to resolve political disputes within Russia.

Perhaps most importantly, the Russian president has broad authority to govern by executive decree. This device quickly evolved into the mainstay of presidential rule in Russia by 1995. Russia specialist Gordon Smith of the University of South Carolina has calculated that President Yeltsin had issued an average of 12 or 13 decrees a month before the clash with parliament in fall 1993, but the number had quintupled to 65 in December 1993. By 1996, following the election of an even more anti-Yeltsin parliament in December 1995, the president had virtually given up attempting to govern with parliament's participation and had resorted to de facto rule by decree. Issuance of presidential decrees had tripled in 1996 by comparison with previous years: in the first seven months of 1996, there were 591 presidential decrees—which retain the force of law unless overridden by a two-thirds vote of both houses of parliament—raising serious questions about the decisionmaking process of such an overloaded system of presidential governance. Two questions arise here: First, who is drafting, and reading, this sea of decrees? How can the Constitutional Court possibly judge them at the rate they are being produced? Second, who is running the government, since it is clear that rule by decree places the center of political gravity on access to the Russian president, who has been seriously ill and physically unfit to govern much of the time. (In the second half of 1996, a sick Yeltsin spent no more than 15 days at work in the Kremlin.) Much of Russian politics thus comes down to lobbying the presidential staff, which is barely mentioned in the constitution. Not surprisingly, in such an unstructured situation, individuals play a disproportionate role in the decisionmaking process. Throughout 1996 two stood out in this respect: Anatoly Chubais, then Yeltsin's chief of staff, and President Yeltsin's daughter Tatyana, who appears to be one of the very few individuals to have the president's confidence. Under these circumstances, Russia's written constitution must be regarded as a poor guide to the actual distribution of political power and the process by which decisions are made.

The Parliament

Parliaments in Russia have had a brief and unhappy history. Established after the Russian Revolution of 1905, Russia's first Duma was unable to persuade the czar to relinquish autocracy. Then, as now, Russian politics centered around the head of state and personal and extralegal access to him. The establishment of Communist power in Russia signaled the end of efforts to introduce significant parliamentary influence on government for three-quarters of a century, until Gorbachev authorized the first relatively free elections to a Soviet parliament in spring 1989. Up to that point, the Supreme Soviet, as the Soviet parliament was styled, was simply a rubber-stamp body for decisions previously made in the higher councils of the Soviet Communist party. Meeting twice a year for several days and without a staff of any note, the Supreme Soviet was manifestly incapable of evolving into a meaningful deliberative body, much less influencing the affairs of state.

The immediate antecedents of the current Russian Duma lay in the free election in spring 1989 of a two-level Soviet parliament, including an umbrella body, the Congress of People's Deputies (1,068 delegates), and the smaller Supreme Soviet

Two members of parliament, Yevgeniya Tishkovskaya and ultranationalist Vladimir Zhirinovsky, engage in an uninhibited "debate" during emergency session called to denounce NATO airstrikes on Bosnian Serbs. Fistfights in the Duma are not uncommon; fines or reprimands are rare.

(542 delegates). According to Soviet-era legislation, the Congress was the supreme agency of government. Yet the unwieldiness of that body, the heavy representation within it of Soviet officials, and in particular the absence of any mechanism to resolve disputes between parliament and the executive meant that this was a highly unstable structure for governance. At first, this mattered little, as parliamentary leaders such as Speaker Ruslan Khasbulatov rallied to Yeltsin's side to defeat the attempted coup d'état by the Communist old order in August 1991. As Russia assumed real independence in 1992, however, major policy differences between president and legislature placed what proved to be unbearable burdens on post-Soviet Russia's constitutional structure. The major issue over which president and parliament split was the scope and pace of

economic reform, begun in January 1992, which was aimed at liberalizing prices and privatizing as much of the old Soviet state-owned economy as quickly as possible. Yeltsin's own vice president, former air force colonel Aleksandr V. Rutskoi, joined the parliamentary opposition in alarm at the impact that the withdrawal of government subsidies was likely to have on the Russian economy's large military-industrial sector.

A perilous confrontation was thus joined. An armed clash seemed to be narrowly averted in March 1993 when Yeltsin withdrew a threat to impose direct presidential rule in exchange for referenda on his rule and policies to be held in April 1993. Although Yeltsin received broad popular support in the four referendum items, the opposition majority in parliament remained unreconciled, and on September 21, 1993, Yeltsin dissolved the parliament by decree. With this admittedly unconstitutional act, Yeltsin triggered a chain of events that led to a violent clash between parliament and president that culminated in the shelling of the Russian White House, home of the parliament, by Yeltsin's troops on October 4. The Clinton Administration, which had cemented its partnership with Yeltsin at a Russian-American summit meeting in Vancouver, Canada, the previous April, tacitly welcomed this act. About 140 people are thought to have died in the fighting and leaders of the opposition, including Khasbulatov and Rutskoi, were sent to jail.

It was on this basis that Russia's current parliament was established in the elections of December 12, 1993. The constitution that was adopted provided for a weak parliament, thereby assuring Yelstin's domination of the governmental structure. Yet the elections themselves were a striking defeat for Yeltsin's political allies. An extreme nationalist group, named the Liberal Democratic party and led by Vladimir Zhirinovsky, captured nearly 23 percent of the vote cast for political parties that were allocated half the seats. Russia's Choice, the president's party, received just 15.5 percent of votes cast for parties. When votes for individual candidates are taken into account, President Yeltsin's strong supporters accounted for less than 16% of seats (70 out of 450), while his strong opponents in Zhirinovsky's party, the Communist party of the Russian Federation and its ally, the Agrarian party, made up nearly one third (145 out of 450). In combination with other, smaller parties and the 31 percent of seats occupied by independents, antigovernment forces could count on frequent majorities in the new parliament.

While Yeltsin could not count on real support from the parliament, neither could the parliament, whose other federal chamber (consisting of members appointed by Yeltsin) was noticeably less hostile to Yeltsin, expect to obtain the kinds of supermajorities needed to wrest control of the government. As long as this situation prevailed, there was a certain stability in relations between the executive and legislative branches. Moreover, Yeltsin's prime minister, the pragmatic power broker Viktor S. Chernomyrdin, who replaced the ideologically inspired market reformer Yegor T. Gaidar in response to parliamentary pressure in December 1992, was much more disposed to work with parliament wherever possible. The years 1994 and 1995 thus saw a number of important acts of cooperation between parliament and president, as a substantial part of a post-Soviet legal infrastructure was developed, including the elaboration of a new criminal code, a code of civil procedure, a tax code and a maritime code.

New Parliament More Hostile to President

Free elections, however, upset the political balance in December 1995. A parliament that was even more hostile to Yeltsin was elected in response to the growing impoverishment of much of Russian society and the prolonged and highly unpopular war in Chechnya. The Communist party, led by presidential aspirant Gennady Zyuganov, increased its vote by half over the previous elections and obtained 22.3 percent of the total. Ultranationalist Zhirinovsky's party receded in relation to Communist gains and received just over 11 percent of the vote, while the government's party, Our Home Is Russia, received just over 10 percent. Economist Grigory Yavlinsky's liberal-reform bloc, Yabloko, received just under 7 percent. Combined with votes for individual candidates and translated into seats in the Duma, Yeltsin's strong opponents now controlled a solid majority of parliamentary seats. Together with splinter groups generally hostile to governmental policy, this meant that the Duma was much closer to obtaining the two-thirds threshold required by the constitution to challenge Yeltsin's government and perhaps—by invoking the constitution's impeachment clause—even the president himself.

The strength of the opposition was reflected in a greater hostility to Yeltsin and a greater willingness to challenge governmental policy. In response, as noted earlier, Yeltsin and his advisers resorted to de facto presidential rule by relying on executive decrees to govern the country. The increasing remove of the governmental process from parliamentary influence led the Duma in mid-November 1996 to approve, by a vote of 344 to 1, a resolution calling for greater parliamentary oversight of the cabinet. Such a measure, because it would entail a change in the constitution, would probably not pass the test of judicial review by Russia's Constitutional Court. It is, however, an accurate indicator of the polarization between parliament and president, of the inability to devise a collaborative approach to problems of governance, and of the fact that, as scholars Joseph L. Nogee and R. Judson Mitchell have noted in their 1997 book, *Russian Politics: The Struggle for a New Order*, Russia has "not yet emerged from the politics of transition."

Political Polarization Is Compounded by Social Polarization

Those States are likely to be well administered in which the middle class is large, and larger if possible than both the other classes, or at any rate than either singly; for the addition of the middle class turns the scale and prevents either of the extremes from being dominant.

—Aristotle, *Politics*, Book IV

The polarization of Russian politics parallels a profound and growing polarization within Russian society, as the winners and losers of Russia's post-Soviet economic transition sense that while some have indeed "won," many, and perhaps the majority of the population, have definitively "lost" in the contest for the allocation of Russia's economic and social resources. A study of Russian poverty in the 1990s by economist Vladimir Mikhalev has concluded that "the lack of an effective safety net capable of alleviating the social hardships of the transition has been an important cause of growing popular disappointment [and] despair...giving rise to the danger of social unrest. The results of the December 1995 parliamentary elections in Russia (where the Communists won a majority of votes) and the collisions in the course of the presidential election [campaign] in 1996 provided vivid evidence of the gravity of political backlashes against the reforms."

Some of the alarming indicators of the economic and social price that much of the Russian population has been paying in recent years include:

➤ A tripling of economic inequality in the first years of the transition: the richest top 10 percent of the population now earns 14 times the income of the poorest 10 percent, compared to 5.4 times as much in 1991; economic inequalities between regions in Russia also rose dramatically, as the ratio of real per capita income between the richest and poorest regions increased from about 8:1 in 1992 to 42:1 by 1994;

➤ The effective collapse of the wage structure: in real terms, the minimum wage had by 1996 fallen to 20 percent of its 1991 level and was equal to just 7 percent of the average wage; moreover, by early 1996, the average real wage was worth 40 percent of its preform level—these losses are compounded by widespread wage arrears, which amounted to nearly one third of the wage bill by early 1996;

➤ The decline of the wages of professionals and engineers, who form the backbone of Russia's aspiring middle class: their wages—led by those of teachers and medical staff—have fallen to levels lower than those of unskilled workers; wage levels in education were 77 percent of the official subsistence minimum in mid-1995, in culture and the arts 74 percent, and in the health-care sector as a whole, 95 percent;

➤ Higher food costs: as a result of declining real wages, the percentage of salary that consumers spent on food rose from 36.1 percent in 1990 to 52 percent in 1995;

➤ A poverty rate commonly estimated at over 50 percent of the Russian population; moreover, working-age adults—that is, the economically active population rather than pensioners (as is commonly assumed)—form the majority of the poor; beyond this, regional data suggest that fewer than 20 percent of households eligible to receive some kind of locally provided social assistance are actually getting it; 80 percent of Russians are thought to have no savings at all;

➤ A decline in male life expectancy, from 63.8 years in 1990 to 58 years in 1995, and an annual excess of deaths over births approaching 800,000, foreshadowing a long-term decline in the Russian population, which over time had grown to become Europe's largest; remarkably, a Russian male teenager of 16 has less chance to reach the age of 60 today (54 percent) than did his greatgrandfather 100 years ago (56 percent);

➤ A more than 10 percent decline in daily calorie intake, from 2,589 in 1990 to 2,310 in 1995 (a daily calorie intake below 2,350 is considered "going hungry" by the UN Food and Agriculture Organization);

➤ A dramatic increase in suicides, from 39,150 in 1990 to 56,136 by 1993, followed by an 11 percent increase the following year, leaving Russia with the third-highest suicide rate in the world; in 1992 and 1993 suicides accounted for nearly one third of Russia's unnatural deaths; between 1990 and 1996, suicides increased by 50 percent.

It should be self-evident from the picture of Russian society that emerges from these trends that economic inequality has increased dramatically in just a few years, that the wage structure of the former middle class has effectively collapsed, and that, even where people have been able to maintain some semblance of subsistence and dignity, they have done so through a sudden, thorough and traumatic change in their working hours and lifestyle. Russian society, in short, is under tremendous stress. A Soviet-era middle class that is growing smaller and increasingly insecure—even as elements of a post-Soviet entrepreneurial class are being established—is most unlikely to serve as the social foundation for stable political democracy in a country where neither the institutions nor the values of democracy have taken very deep root. Russia's post-Soviet electoral history bears this point out.

Russia's Electoral History

Perhaps the most positive feature of recent Russian politics, and one of the few that bodes well for the country's eventual democratic evolution, is the fact that free and regular elections have been held, on schedule, since 1989, on the presidential, parliamentary, provincial and local levels. As of early 1997, nine major sets of popular votes had been held in Russia, dating from the Soviet era in early 1989 (see pages 28 and 29).

What can be said about the signficance of this apparently impressive electoral history? First, it is positive in itself that the electoral principle has been adopted, and rather consistently practiced, in Russian politics since the late 1980s. As legislative and especially presidential elections are repeated, the precedent thereby set will tend to raise a progressively higher barrier to those who might seek to simply seize and appropriate political power. It should be noted, however, that the acid test of the durability of electoral procedure has yet to be passed in Russia: that is, elections which involve a transfer of effective political authority. As has been shown, the two victories for Yeltsin's opponents in the parliamentary elections in December 1993 and December 1995 had little impact on fundamental governmental policy. Indeed, the momentous decision to invade Chechnya in December 1994 was made without any reference to the Duma at all. Moreover, the second Russian presidential election in summer 1996 confirmed the incumbent in office in circumstances that raised serious questions about the fairness of the procedure. The crucial test for Russia's adherence to elections as the basis for forming a government will thus occur at the *next* scheduled presidential election in 2000 (they could be held sooner if Yeltsin dies in office or is incapacitated). A

Nine Major Popular Elections

- ✔ MARCH 1989: The entire U.S.S.R., Russia included, elected a Congress of People's Deputies in the freest elections since 1917. In spite of many protected seats, a number of leading Communist party officials were defeated, sending shock waves throughout the party establishment. Fully 88 percent of the successful candidates were elected for the first time to public office. Voter turnout was 87 percent in Russia.

- ✔ 1990: Soviet republics held their own elections, in the process legitimizing nationalist politics, especially in the western and southern republics (the Baltic states, the Caucasus states and Ukraine). Russian voter turnout was 77 percent.

- ✔ MARCH 1991: Gorbachev and Yeltsin conducted competing referenda on the Soviet and Russian levels, respectively. Sixty-one percent of the Soviet electorate (and 76 percent of actual voters) supported a vaguely worded concept for a reformed U.S.S.R. while a comparable percentage in Russia (52.5 percent of the electorate and 70 percent of actual voters) endorsed the idea of electing a Russian president by direct popular vote, thereby legitimizing Yeltsin's Russian challenge to Gorbachev and his concept of the union. Turnout for Gorbachev's referendum was about 80 percent throughout the U.S.S.R.; 75 percent of the Russian electorate turned out for Yeltsin's referendum.

- ✔ JUNE 1991: Yeltsin was elected president of Russia with nearly 60 percent of the vote in a six-man race. (Gorbachev, in a fundamental miscalculation, never submitted himself to a direct popular vote for statewide office.) Turnout was 75 percent.

- ✔ APRIL 1993: In a four-point referendum, Yeltsin received broad majority support for his presidency and policies in the midst of his political conflict with the Russian parliament. Turnout was 64 percent.

✔ **DECEMBER 1993:** Yeltsin received a major setback as his political opponents garnered half the seats in the Duma, less than three months after his tanks had shelled the Russian White House. Voter turnout continued to decline, to 55 percent.

✔ **DECEMBER 1995:** Yeltsin and his government received an even greater shock as the progovernment party, Our Home Is Russia, led by Prime Minister Chernomyrdin, received just 10 percent of the vote in nationwide parliamentary elections. Turnout increased to 64.4 percent.

✔ **JUNE AND JULY 1996:** In a remarkable comeback, Yeltsin, whose popularity was in single digits earlier in the year, outpolled Communist party leader Gennady Zyuganov 35.3 to 32 percent in the first round of presidential elections. Former General Aleksandr Lebed, whose campaign was financed and led by key Yeltsin aides, drew 14.5 percent of the vote and thereby guaranteed Yeltsin's first-place finish. Yeltsin immediately awarded the post of national security adviser to Lebed, who in effect threw his supporters behind Yeltsin, helping the latter to cement a 54-40 percent victory over Zyuganov in the two-man second-round race in July. Turnout jumped to nearly 70 percent in both rounds of elections. (Lebed would be dismissed in October 1996 after negotiating an armistice to the Chechen war and evincing clear presidential ambitions himself.)

✔ **SEPTEMBER–JANUARY 1996/97:** Forty-five gubernatorial and five other regional elections took place in which governors were chosen by direct popular vote instead of presidential appointment. The ballots were a disappointment for the government: a majority of pro-Yeltsin incumbents were defeated.

number of signs in the spring of 1996—such as Yeltsin aide Maj. Gen. Aleksandr V. Korzhakov suggesting postponement of the June 1996 presidential election—indicated that the prospect of expelling the incumbent government from office could meet with serious resistance, throwing the country, and with it Russia's electoral prospects, into upheaval.

Second, however encouraging Russia's nascent electoral tradition may be, the fact remains that the single most important political conflict in post-Soviet Russia—the impasse between president and parliament in 1993—was resolved by force of arms rather than by vote or compromise. The subsequent constitution, enshrining a presidentially dominant political order, reflects that brutal fact. As a result, the elected parliaments have had little real influence upon governmental policy. As has been observed, a critical test for democracy is not just the holding of elections but meaningful, if indirect, constituent influence on the state. It is clear that the severe imbalance between executive and legislative agencies of government in Russia hinders the evolution of Russia's democratic possibilities. A freely and fairly elected parliament that broadly represents the spectrum of popular opinion but has no real impact on the composition and course of the government is hardly an improvement on the rubber stamp Supreme Soviet of Communist days. Indeed, to the extent that the concept of democracy is identified by the population with such hollow institutions, democracy itself will be the loser. To compound matters, the largest party represented in the parliament—the Russian Communist party, whose presidential candidate received 40 percent of the vote—is far from being unambiguously committed to democratic procedure.

Third, the early pattern of Russia's elections, presidential as well as parliamentary, demonstrates that in current Russian conditions the extension of electoral participation and structural market reform in the economy—that is "democratization" and "marketization"—tend to proceed at the expense of one another rather than in tandem. A large percentage of the Russian population, indeed perhaps the majority, which has not been able to adapt to Russia's post-Soviet market economy, has three times expressed its dissatisfaction with the direction of government policy: by humiliating progovernment parties at the legislative polls in 1993 and 1995 and by a disturbing generational split during the presidential election in summer 1996. A majority of the Russian population over the age of 45 voted for Communist candidate Zyuganov in the presidential runoff of July 1996, while a majority under 45 voted for Yeltsin. Such a split need not endanger the stability of the system. After all, revolts and riots are seldom made by the older generations. But it does raise questions about the capacity of Russian politicians and Russia's political institutions to establish a political order that is responsive to broad sectors of the population, that is based on tolerance and compromise for the sake of the system rather than on efforts to seize (or maintain seizure of) the state for the ends of one faction and its clients.

Yeltsin Capitalized on Perks

Fourth, the Russian presidential election of 1996 was far from the free and fair vote proclaimed by the government and its diplomatic supporters in Washington and elsewhere abroad. This is not to say that the vote was a sham, or to deny that Yeltsin conducted a vigorous and effective campaign, especially compared with his chief rivals in the Communist and liberal-democratic camp. Yeltsin was able to polarize the choice presented to the Russian electorate: choose him and vote for the future, or vote Zyuganov and bring back the dark, totalitarian past. Such tactics helped Yeltsin edge out Zyuganov in the multicandidate first round in June and in the two-man runoff in July. Of course, Yeltsin enjoyed, and created for himself, a number of advantages through the direct and indirect use of his governmental powers that seriously distorted the choices before the voters. These were not simply the "powers of incumbency" that so many Western observers complacently attributed to such tactics. Yeltsin enjoyed something close to a monopoly in the television and much of the press coverage of the campaign. Some of this was accomplished through the apparently voluntary support of Yeltsin by many journalists who felt themselves threatened in the event of a Communist victory. In a number of cases, it turned out that key corporations under clear governmental influence, such as the gas giant Gazprom with very close connections to Prime Minister Chernomyrdin, had bought major shares of key television networks (such as NTV—"Independent Television"). Most blatantly, the Yeltsin government funded and guided the candidacy of General Lebed, whose votes in the first round assured Yeltsin's narrow edge over Zyuganov. (A difference of 1.7 percent of the vote would have placed Zyuganov ahead of Yeltsin.) Moreover, the comments of some of Yeltsin's closest aides cast serious doubt on the government's commitment to the electoral process. Although Korzhakov, the most notorious among these, was later fired, the government was apparently prepared, if only as a contingency, to circumvent the polls in the event of an impending defeat. In short, the 1996 presidential election result is a highly fragile precedent by which to judge Russia's electoral future.

Finally, whatever Russia's electoral course, it must be remembered that elections, however free, without reliable means for representatives to influence policy, do not form the basis for democracy, much less constitutional government. For now, there are few ways by which the constitutionally established agencies of government, even within the executive branch, can affect the decisionmaking process without direct access to the president's staff. The fact that so much attention in Russia and throughout the world is focused on the state of Yeltsin's health suggests just how little confidence there is in the capacity of Russia's post-Soviet institutions to guide the ship of state through the admittedly uncharted waters of the post-Communist transformation.

The System of Presidential Authority

The most significant line in the Russian constitution is perhaps Article 83, Section i, which states simply that the president "shall form his administrative staff." This provision, which was intended to provide for the routine administrative needs of the president's office, has turned out to be the operative key to understanding high politics in Russia. In brief, faced with an unsympathetic parliament, weak governmental ministries and his own disinclination to systematize the decisionmaking process, President Yeltsin has developed an informal staff structure that has become the linchpin of Russian politics. In many respects it duplicates the formal structure of government ministries and agencies. (Remarkably, it seems that there has been a major *increase* in the number of Russian bureaucrats since the disintegration of the U.S.S.R.)

In Russia's superpresidentialist system, the president's word is decisive. Access to the president is therefore critical in advancing the agenda of any government office. What Yeltsin's office has devised is a structure of presidential access that makes nearly all governmental and extragovernmental agencies compete with each other for the scarce and precious commodity of presidential time and/or imprimatur. In this respect, the real decisionmaking structure finds Yeltsin in the position of czar: nothing of importance happens without presidential approval; moreover, access to the president is all. In principle, such a system, authoritarian as it is, can work as a vehicle of governance, but it requires a highly competent, informed, skillful and interventionist chief executive to function. (Otto von Bismarck's chancellorship, 1871–90, in Imperial Germany and Henry A. Kissinger's administration of U.S. foreign policy during the presidency of Richard M. Nixon, 1969–73, come to mind as models.) In the absence of such a political virtuoso, however, the political system tends to decompose, as all actors await responses from the top that seldom come. In this respect, Yeltsin's personal disinclination to attend to the administration of government, reinforced by his lengthy absences due to illness, is exactly the wrong match of political personality to political system. Yeltsin's brief ally and now putative successor, Lebed, accurately characterized the consequences of this mismatch in early 1997: "Today we have an authoritarian system of power. Until the president at the top does something, then nothing happens in this pyramid."

What happens instead is that government is run for the most part by informal and usually covert cabals of claimants to the resources and protection of the state, who are able to obtain access to the presidential chain of command, frequently through the outright purchase of officials' time and accord. U.S. diplomat Thomas E. Graham, who is responsible for analyzing Russian internal affairs at the U.S. Embassy in Moscow, characterized this system in late 1995 in an article published in a leading Russian newspaper as "clan" politics, in which an oligarchic collection of economic interests struggle for access to the president and thus state resources in order "to engineer a political stability that would insure their hold on power and the country's financial resources." The contesting clans include a group of oil and gas industrialists under the aegis of Prime Minister Chernomyrdin; a "Moscow group" under the auspices of Mayor Yuri Luzhkov and based upon the city's banking and real estate interests; a military-industrial and security circle responsible for the war in Chechnya, led in part by Korzhakov, Yeltsin's close personal adviser and security chief until June 1996; an "agrarian" group controlling the mainly unreformed Soviet-era farm sector; and a group of "Westernizers," such as Yeltsin's first deputy premier in charge of the economy, Anatoly Chubais, whose power stems from their involvement in the privatization of the Russian economy and their access to Western financial institutions, like the World Bank and the International Monetary Fund, which have played important roles in sustaining the Russian state budget through difficult times. The principal mechanism by which these clans' interests is advanced is the promulgation of presidential decrees, which often establish tax or import/export advantages. It is quite obvious that with well over 500 such decrees issued in each of the last two years, when Yeltsin was too ill to govern for extended periods of time, the Russian president has in effect ceded enormous economic and political power to private interests, or clans, whose access to the Russian government is mediated by his staff.

These "clans," Graham wrote, "contain few staunch supporters of democracy, and none of the clans are devoted to democratic ideals, despite public assurances to the contrary." Indeed, elections "present a danger to [this] elite because even though they retain the levers of power, they understand less and less what is going on in society." In principle, a healthy and activist president able to impose the general interests of Russian society on the Russian political process might be in a position to advance the interests of society and of the system as a whole. In practice, his absence has meant that, with a presidential cabal embedded within a superpresidentialist constitution, Russian politics has become the prisoner of a new post-Soviet economic and financial oligarchy that has seen the interests of its individual sectors, and often the pecuniary interests of its leading individuals, become the focal point of the political system. "Thus," the Nobel prize-winning Russian novelist Aleksandr Solzhenitsyn has concluded, "a stable and tight oligarchy of 150–200 people, including the most cunning representatives of the top and middle strata of the former Communist ruling structure, along with numerous nouveaux riches who amassed their recent fortunes through banditry, has been established." Alessandra Stanley, *The New York Times* Moscow correspondent, concurs: "In post-Communist Russia, the politburo has been replaced by a deal-making oligarchy—the dozen or so powerful, fiercely competitive businessmen who run the banks, oil companies and news organizations, and who banded together to bankroll President Boris N. Yeltsin's reelection."

3

The Crisis of the Russian State

The authority of the Russian government today is, unfortunately, at a low level. This impedes the establishment of order in the country and threatens the security of Russia.

—President Yeltsin in a national radio address, April 10, 1997.

STABLE DEMOCRACIES, as was pointed out earlier, are based on functioning market economies, the rule of law and competent governance. By the latter is meant a system of state administration that is able to perform adequately the minimum necessary tasks of any government, democratic or otherwise. These involve, most importantly:

(a) the ability to collect taxes sufficient to finance the agencies of the state (including the revenue service itself);

(b) civilian control over the military;

(c) control over the external borders of the state;

(d) the capacity to suppress internal rebellion; and

(e) the capacity to enforce the law of the land.

In Russia today, the inability of its government to raise adequate tax revenue, itself a reflection of the political deadlock just depicted, has compounded its incapacity to govern effectively in many other spheres, including those listed above. In order to gauge the effectiveness of the Russian state, one must examine several key areas of governmental responsibility, including economic developments, the explosion of organized crime, the status of the Russian military and Russian science policy, including the nuclear sector.

The Economy

A 1996 report by the United Nations International Labor Organization concluded starkly: "There should be no pretense. The Russian economy and the living standards of the Russian population have suffered the worst peacetime setbacks of any industrialized nation in history." Consider the following:

✓ Russia has experienced an economic decline in the industrial sector in each of the past six years that is as much as twice as bad as the decline the United States endured during the worst year of the Great Depression in the 1930s: in 1996, the economic decline continued, though at a slower pace (an estimated 6 percent decline in the industrial sector). Zero percent growth at best is projected for 1997 and 1998.

✓ The Russian government has lacked the necessary political strength to bring about genuine structural change in the economy. In 1994, for example, fully half the Russian government's program to stimulate investment was never implemented. According to Herbert Levine of the PlanEcon research institute, fixed investment in Russia declined by 9 percent in 1996. To cite one example, in the first three quarters of 1996, just 12 of 411 construction projects envisaged by the government's investment budget were completed. At 20 percent of the sites, no work was carried out at all. None of the 77 construction projects in agriculture, which received only 20 percent of allocated investment, was finished.

✓ Corrupt and incompetent financial administration, as well as poor investor confidence, has led to capital flight abroad

Moscow, January 13, 1997: Bryansk region teachers, who are paid less than unskilled workers, demonstrate to collect unpaid wages.

Reuters/Alexander Natruskin/Archive Photos

that is estimated conservatively at between $61 billion (according to the prestigious London-based Economist Intelligence Unit) and $89 billion (according to the World Bank). The investment firm Deutsche Morgan Grenfell has estimated that capital flight in 1996 was $22.3 billion, or 5 percent of Russia's gross domestic product (GDP)and a third of total private savings. Net capital outflow is estimated at $3.5 billion for the first quarter of 1997. (By contrast, direct foreign investment in Russia totaled no more than $6 billion between 1989 and the first half of 1996.)

✓ The central government has struggled at times to collect as much as half the tax revenue needed to finance an admittedly unrealistic budget, according to the Russian Finance Ministry. In the first quarter of 1997, tax revenues were 58 percent of those budgeted. Whereas 1992 state revenue amounted to 44.2 percent of GDP, by mid-1996 that figure had fallen to 29 percent, underscoring the fiscal crisis of the Russian state.

✓ Workers who depend upon state-financed enterprises for a living have experienced lengthy delays in receiving their wages. A Russian survey conducted in late 1996 disclosed that only 30 percent of wages in Russia were paid on time and in full in 1996, down from 45 percent in 1995. Thirty-one percent of wages were delayed, and 39 percent of wages were simply not paid at all, compared to 38 and 17 percent, respectively, in 1995. Those most likely to be affected were manual workers, inhabitants of rural areas and those living in Siberia and the Russian Far East. High-ranking government officials and managers, as well as residents of Moscow and St. Petersburg, were least likely to be affected.

In mid-1996, two Swiss management firms published parallel studies of the 49 leading economies of the world, by which they meant those most likely to affect the world's future economic growth. Both—the Lausanne-based International Institute for Management Development and the Geneva-based World Economic Forum—ranked Russia dead last in economic competitiveness. The organizations reviewed over 100 criteria for each country, including openness to foreign trade, government budgets and regulations, development of financial markets, flexibility of labor markets, quality of infrastructure, technology, business management and judicial institutions. The World Economic Forum concluded in its justification of Russia's lowest ranking: "Russia is isolated from world markets, taxation is high and unstable and there is a general disdain for the infrastructure, technology and management." For such reasons, which have more to do with the political and legal context of the Russian economy than with Russia's intrinsic economic possibilities, the Economist Intelligence Unit has regularly listed Russia as the riskiest foreign investment destination among countries that it tracks.

Positive Signs of Improvement

There are more-optimistic views of the state of the Russian economy and the course of Russian reform. Russia's private sector—which largely escapes the official economic statistics, based as they are on the old Soviet state sector—is expanding rapidly and now accounts for perhaps half of Russia's GDP, nearly triple the figure in 1991. Two thirds of domestic retail trade took place outside of state channels as early as 1993, compared with one third in 1991. By mid-1996, more than 100,000 state-owned businesses had been privatized, joining a million registered new small businesses. And inflation, which hovered in four digits for 1992, had been reduced to less than 10 percent per month by mid-1994 and less than 1 percent per month by mid-1996 (it was 21.8 percent for the whole of 1996; 1997 inflation is projected at 12 percent). There are other structural signs that reform is proceeding apace: services are now contributing more to the Russian economy (50 percent) than manufacturing, suggesting that Russia is developing the beginnings of a sectoral profile associated with advanced economies; unemployment has been significantly lower than expected (9 percent for 1996), perhaps reflecting the beginnings of a functioning labor market. Such developments have led futurologists Daniel Yergin and Thane Gustafson, authors of the 1993 book *Russia 2010: And What It Means for the World*, to write that "the new market economy...is developing in Russia much faster than is generally recognized." "Elements of Russian capitalism are already in place. Early in the next century, people may be talking about 'a Russian economic miracle.'"

The Rise of Post-Soviet Russian Crime

To a certain extent, the picture of unprecedented decline in the traditional Soviet economy and the rise of a vibrant new private and service economy are two sides of the same coin. Indeed, it would be fatal to the prospects of Russian economic reform if there were an increase or even a stabilization of obsolescent industrial and military production. Yet the debility of Russia's public institutions has meant that elements of the new economic and social order have been distorted to an extent unforeseen by those in Russia and the West who have helped design Russia's economic transformation. Most dramatically, organized crime has stepped into the breach of state authority and dominated the privatization of Russian industry, which is one of the most highly advertised success stories of the Russian government. In what Bernard Guetta of the French daily *Le Monde* has termed the "biggest holdup in history," Russia's criminal "mafia," in combination with many in the old Communist elite, has taken over much of the economically valuable property in Russia and with consequences—such as massive capital flight—that are far from helpful to the future productiveness of the Russian economy. Russia's Tass-Krim press agency has reported that the Russian mafia has "privatized [between] 50 and 80 percent of all shops, depots, hotels, and services in Moscow." According to Yeltsin adviser Piotr Filipov, who heads the Center for Political and Economic Analysis, criminal elements control 40,000 privatized enterprises and collect protection money from 80 percent of the country's banks and private enterprises. In August 1995, the Russian Ministry of Internal Affairs conservatively estimated that criminal groups

A terrorist bomb, which destroyed a trolleybus in central Moscow in July 1996, contributed to the malaise of a capital in the grip of an organized crime wave.

control over 400 banks and 47 financial exchanges. Assassination of uncooperative bankers and businessmen has become commonplace, as have contract murders in general. Infiltration of the financial sector has helped to provide the assets needed to control much of Russian industry. In April 1997, Lawrence H. Summers, U.S. Deputy Secretary of the Treasury, stated that three fourths of Moscow shops paid security firms for protection and that Russian businessmen routinely had to pay bribes to secure import or export licenses, lease commercial space or register their firms. Illegal payments designed to circumvent regulatory problems amount to as much as 15 percent of Russian wage costs, according to Summers.

There are some striking and disturbing parallels between what is occurring in Russia today and the conditions that led to the rise of the Italian mafia in Sicily toward the end of the nineteenth century. In both the Sicily of that time and contemporary Russia, a very small elite—the landowning class in late nineteenth–century Sicily and the Communist party in Soviet Russia—controlled almost all property, social privileges and political power, including the use of force.

In both countries this feudal power structure collapsed very rapidly under the pressure of the forces of modernization. The details of this process are less important than the consequences: i.e., the rapid breakup of property holdings, so that almost overnight these were in many individual hands instead of a few; the disintegration of traditional political authority, so that there was no effective legal and police protection of the new social and economic order; the sudden loss of jobs by military or paramilitary forces, who now found themselves in need of gainful employment. Thus, both the demand for and the supply of security increased rapidly and at the same time in both late-nineteenth century Sicily and contemporary Russia. The result, in both cases, was the rise of a powerful mafia, at heart an industry of private protection or private security. Unfortunately, in Russia today, in contrast to the disciplined criminality of La Cosa Nostra—the Italian mafia—there are virtually no accepted rules or limitations on the behavior of organized crime. Russia's greatest deficit is one of security, and its public institutions have proved unable to fill this critical gap.

In a very important sense, then, Russia today is like Sicily, but a Sicily without the rest of Italy behind it to limit the scope of the mafia's power. Russian economic crime is parasitic, not productive. For the most part, Russia's new rich have accumulated their wealth by exploiting privileged access to resources they have paid precious little to acquire or develop. Under these circumstances, tremendous profits for individuals or firms may be obtained by selling items on the world market at dumping prices, which still bring income far exceeding any investments already made. On the whole, those profits, beyond the funds needed to sustain a sumptuous lifestyle within Russia and to maintain this parasitic type of economy, are being invested outside the country. Ironically, it may be the case that Russian capital, in spite of the vastly superior resource base of Russia's economy, is contributing more to the development of the Chinese economy than it is to its own. The criminal class in Russia lacks the confidence in the country's legal prospects that is prerequisite to large-scale productive investment in the nation's economic future.

The Military

The extreme difficulties that the Russian military has experienced in subduing Chechnya, where the Russian army suffered more casualties in the first month than it did in the six months following the December 1979 invasion of Afghanistan from which it eventually withdrew in defeat and humiliation, underscores the fragility of the power of the contemporary Russian state. Many of the reasons for the numerous setbacks encountered by the Russian army, reminiscent of the U.S.S.R.'s difficult campaign against Finland in the Soviet-Finnish War of 1939–40, are already clear. They include disastrous military tactics (relying on tanks to take the city of Grozny, the same mistake the Serbs made in Slovenia in June 1991), reflecting the failure (or inability) to execute Russia's new military doctrine, which places a premium on highly maneuverable rapid deployment forces; poorly trained troops, many of whom had never exercised together (some marine units had to be brought in from Vladivostok, whereas comparable units were also available in the nearby Black Sea fleet); lack of coordination between units and services; low morale and insufficient combat readiness; strong divisions of view among the military high command (comparable to those that undermined the coup d'état of August 1991) and, consequently, lack of unified military support for the operation.

In fact, many of these characteristics of Russia's armed forces were clear to careful observers many months before the invasion of Chechnya. The unexpected and unplanned collapse of the Soviet army, from 3.5 million to 4 million troops in 1990–91 to a Russian armed force of fewer than 1.3 million today, has been part of a broader picture that underscores the disintegration of the once vaunted Red Army (now mainly the Russian army) as a capable combat organization. Consider the following evidence:

(a) It took the Russian army nearly one year to organize an expeditionary force of 15,000 troops to police the frontier between Tajikistan and Afghanistan.

(b) Military procurement has fallen catastrophically. Whereas in the early 1980s the U.S.S.R. produced 100 different *kinds* of military aircraft, by 1993 the Russian government purchased just 17 military aircraft of all types. In 1996, the Russian military purchased not a single new combat aircraft.

(c) Today, a typical Russian air force pilot receives at best 23-50 hours per year of flying time, versus a minimum of 120 for an average Atlantic alliance–country pilot.

(d) In part as a consequence of the state's loss of the power to collect tax revenue (combined with the general institutional chaos set in motion during the last months of Gorbachev's tenure in office), it has also lost control over the military. (For example, in August 1996 the Defense Ministry apparently received none of its allocated funds from the federal government, and just 4.4 percent in July.) Moreover, as the

Chechnya operation shows, the military high command has also lost considerable control over its own subordinate units.

(e) Russian Defense Ministry officials anticipate that most officers will quit military service when their contracts expire in late 1997. Sixty-one percent of the military officers suffer from chronic financial problems, with 29 percent living below the poverty line.

As a result, the Russian ground forces are only suitable for internal use—and even there with considerable difficulties, as Chechnya shows—or against a third-rate power. They lack the capacity to project power or to engage in sustained combat operations against a competent, modern military force, such as that of Turkey. Yury Baturin, secretary of the Russian president's advisory Defense Council, concluded in February 1997 that the army was "in a critical state....If things continue in this way for another two years we could have a navy without ships, an air force without aircraft and [a] defense industry unable to make weapons."

The Condition of Russian Science

If the military have not been spared the effects of the general collapse of state authority in Russia, it is little wonder that the former Soviet scientific establishment is in a struggle for survival as well. When the U.S.S.R. collapsed, the scientific community fell into disarray. Today, its very survival is at risk. The Organization for Economic Cooperation and Development (OECD), composed of virtually all the industrialized free-market states, has described the condition of research and development in Russia as being one of "profound crisis." This reflects both the disintegration of a previously integrated scientific network across the territory of the former U.S.S.R. as well as the extreme poverty of the contemporary Russian state. Severe cuts in state spending on science have meant that scientific institutes, including prestigious ones, struggle simply to pay their electric bills and salaries. Wages are often paid months behind schedule. As a result, as much as one fifth of the 60,000 scientists who have skills in electronics, rocketry or other fields useful to nuclear-weapons programs have abandoned their research laboratories in favor of more-lucrative opportunities in the private sector at home, as well as abroad. Of an estimated 950,000 people working in scientific research and development in Russia in 1991, 200,000–300,000 are thought to have left the system altogether. The youngest and most talented are leading the way.

Less than $250 million was devoted to basic scientific research in the Russian government's 1994 budget. Much of that money, in fact, was never spent on the purposes for which it was intended. Overall, state financing for the Academy of Sciences and its numerous institutes, observatories, expeditions, libraries, publishers, etc., has declined by as much as 80 percent over the last several years. Senior scientists at Russia's most prestigious institutes can earn as little as the equivalent of $10 per day (which means that a typical scientist cannot afford on his monthly salary a round-trip ticket between Novosibirsk—a leading scientific center—and Moscow). All told, between 1989 and 1993, the number of people employed in science in all of the countries of the former U.S.S.R. decreased by more than one million. The dismal material conditions and prospects also mean that for the most part talented young people are simply no longer attracted to science as a vocation. This has happened in spite of the fact that, in dollar terms, the expense of conducting scientific research in Russia is about 1/20th of what it costs in the United States.

In the area of nuclear energy, one can only be amazed that another Chernobyl (the worst nuclear disaster in history) has not happened. The Siberian Chemical Combine known as Tomsk-7 has accumulated 23,000 containers of nuclear materials—plutonium and enriched uranium—from obsolete nuclear warheads which are stored in conditions that the Russian government's Security Council described in late 1994 as "extremely unfavorable." The drastic deterioration of wages in the Russian Ministry of Atomic Energy has led to a number of alarming developments since 1992, including strikes by scientific and engineering personnel begun in 1993 because of

Reuters/Viktor Korotayev/Archive Photos

Ignoring safety measures, many factories dump high-radiation waste in areas around Moscow. Two inspectors check the radiation level at an unauthorized dump.

months of delay in the payment of salaries. Such stoppages have since become common: in 1996 it was reported that delays of two to six months in wage payments were common in the nuclear industry. In late 1996 the director of the Russian Federal Nuclear Center in Snezhinsk, Vladimir Nechai, committed suicide in despair over shortfalls in state funding of such magnitude that he concluded he could no longer ensure the safety of the operations or pay the staff.

Moreover, in 1993, 11 attempts to steal uranium from nuclear facilities were averted. There were also 900 instances in which illegal penetrations of closed nuclear facilities were cut short, and 700 instances in which employees tried to take out secret documents and were caught. All such attempts were made by employees with a thorough knowledge of the technology concerned. Finally, it is an open secret that the safety standards of Russia's nuclear industry, as well as those of all Russia's former-Soviet neighbors, are set by the available budgetary resources rather than by internationally accepted minimum criteria, which are deemed too costly to enforce. The post-Soviet nuclear industry is a time bomb waiting to explode.

In Summary

The Russian government is failing to perform some of the elementary functions of governance and in the process jeopardizing not only Russia's democratic prospects but the essential coherence of society. That male life expectancy in Russia has now fallen to 58 years, and that deaths will exceed births in Russia for the long foreseeable future, are just two of the most dramatic indices of the social devastation and despair that have taken root in post-Soviet Russia. Russia's government, having contributed substantially to this social catastrophe by imposing market-type reforms upon a society that was unprepared for them, has proven itself incapable of asserting a minimal political grip on the challenges afflicting both state and society.

Another result has been the devolution of substantial real economic and political powers from the central, Moscow-based Russian state to Russia's numerous federal regions, which have proved able to withhold large sums of taxes owed to the central government, thereby further jeopardizing its ability to govern. In 1996, not one of the Russian Federation's 89 regions had received the federal funds needed to pay pensions and salaries for essential workers. In return, just 10 regions had delivered their required share of tax revenue to Moscow. In the long run, a negotiated and stable transfer of power from the center to the regions is a potentially positive development, both for the coherence of the Russian state as well as the prospects for a more democratic form of government. It should be apparent from the map that a country as vast as Russia cannot be realistically governed from one central point. Yet until the central government can focus its energies on performing at least the minimal functions of governance reasonably well, this emergent federalism will remain an accidental, chaotic and in the end counterproductive phenomenon. In the final analysis, order precedes justice: while a just order will tend to be more durable (not to mention preferable) than an unjust one, there can be no justice on a societywide scale without a minimum degree of order in the affairs of state and society. Societies, as individuals, thirst for security, even when they desire freedom. That security *will* be provided, as the history of the Sicilian and now Russian mafias indicates. But who will provide it, and at what cost?

4

Does Russia Have a Democratic Future?

"Ya ot dvadtsatogo veka ustal."
(I am exhausted from the twentieth century.)
—Lead verse in a 1991 poem by Georgi Skorov

THE PRECEDING analysis suggests that Russia's democratic prospects are problematic at best. In terms of meeting the preconditions for the establishment and maintenance of stable democracy, Russia faces serious obstacles. In spite of the regular holding of elections, many basic conditions for democratic governance have yet to be established. As several British students of Russia's electoral history have written in their 1997 book, *How Russia Votes*, "democracy is not only about deciding who governs but also about how a country is governed." In Russia's first five years of post-Communist government, it has yet to establish the rule of law, an obvious prerequisite of democracy. President Yeltsin is essentially unaccountable in his authority; parliament and the courts are virtually impotent in respect to executive power. Momentous decisions, like that to invade Chechnya, remain the stuff of Yeltsin's inner circle of favorites. Indeed, the deterioration of Russia's formal constitutional order into an oligarchic political economy based on the sectoral and even individual interests of powerful economically based clans has seriously degraded the already limited capacity of the Russian state to grapple with key issues of public order and policy. U.S. diplomat Graham has written that "there are very few committed supporters of democracy in the clans. Democratic procedures, including elections, are mostly seen as weapons in the struggle for power."

As a consequence, the primary political challenge for Russia today is not the development of democracy as practiced in the North Atlantic world but the establishment of a minimally competent civilian state, one that can raise adequate taxes, control the military, enforce the law, police the borders and, in general, put the interests of the state above those of its component parts. Without a functioning system of public administration, which must rest on a relatively broad consensus on the purposes and policies of government within Russia's political class, it is hard to see how the legal and economic components of democratic government can be laid. Moreover, as long as the Russian state fails to fulfill the elementary functions of government, the ensuing disorder will tend to discredit the very idea of democracy that is formally embraced by the Russian government. Polls of Russian public opinion and political attitudes imply that leaders who can associate the prospect of democracy with security—political, social, economic and personal—stand a good chance of forming a winning electoral coalition. Unfortunately, Russia's leaders have not shown themselves up to developing the promise implied by much of Russian public opinion.

Where does Russia stand in the second half of 1997 and where is it likely to head? In *Russia 2010*, Yergin and Gustafson examine a range of alternative political and economic futures for Russia, ranging from the progressive decomposition of the

With real wages falling and living costs soaring, agricultural workers held a protest rally in Moscow in April 1996. Holding a banner with Lenin's portrait, they shouted antigovernment slogans.

Reuters/Viktor Korotayev/Archive Photos

state to outright disintegration, military coup and economic recovery. Interestingly, the authors are much more confident about what cannot happen than what might. Given the triple collapse of the Soviet system—the disintegration of the Communist political system, the centrally planned economy and the empire—it is simply not possible for a highly centralized and integrated Soviet-type country to be reestablished. It is much more difficult to say which of a variety of political-economic scenarios is more rather than less probable. This is so in part because the very weakness of Russia's post-Soviet institutions makes even the simple projection of the present into the short-term future a hazardous undertaking.

Yergin and Gustafson's analysis of Russia's possible futures proceeds from the assumption that, since there is no way back to the command economy, some kind of capitalism lies in store for Russia. It should be noted, however, that capitalist economies have proved compatible with a broad variety of highly authoritarian governments, ranging from Fascist Premier Benito Mussolini's Italy (1922–43) to President Augusto

Pinochet's Chile (1974–90), contemporary Singapore and even China.

'Muddling Down'

Where does Russia stand today, then? Yergin and Gustafson begin with a scenario they call muddling down, which comes close to being a political snapshot of Russia today. Its chief characteristics include: (a) a weak Russian central government; (b) a fierce competition for power, revenues and property; (c) a relatively free political atmosphere (reflecting in part the vacuum of authority left in the wake of the Soviet collapse); (d) a weak and contentious association of former Soviet republics, which can neither live with each other politically nor live without each other economically; (e) a state and industrial economy in decline; and (f) a demoralized and disorganized coercive apparatus (that is, the military and the police).

This "muddled" system roughly describes the Russian political-economic system in the late-1990s. Parts of the system may be dynamic, such as the economy's service sector, but overall it suffers from an inability to produce and implement important political-economic decisions. At best, this is a transitional order. Its durability will depend in substantial part on whether Russia can avoid further major shocks to the political and social order, such as the destruction of the Russian parliament in October 1993, another large-scale use of force as in Chechnya, or mass strikes provoked by sustained nonpayment of wages. Ironically, the apparent stability that Russia has enjoyed since late 1993 rests largely upon the fact that a weak and incapable state has proved a highly satisfactory outcome for the economic clans and criminal networks that have been able to exploit the chaos of the post-Soviet period to enrich themselves by plundering the nation's wealth. Russia would enter a very dangerous period were the government to undertake a crusade to defeat large-scale economic crime: the state's police and judicial agencies are not strong enough to win such an undertaking—most police could not be sure of the security of their own families in such an eventuality—and the ensuing instability could make the reverberations of Russia's defeat in Chechnya pale by comparison. Under these circumstances, Russia's political leaders will have to choose their battles carefully.

Yet without adequate sources of revenue to reassert control over the police and the law-enforcement establishment in general, even strategically chosen efforts are likely to fail. Without a political authority that is able to secure property rights, maintain a stable currency and shape but not unduly intervene in economic development, Russia will not be able to exploit for the benefit of the country as a whole its impressive foundation of natural resources, a highly educated (and low-wage) population, a high level of basic scientific and technological knowledge, a nationwide transportation and communications infrastructure, as well as enormous pent-up demand for consumer goods and services. For these advantages to materialize, enormous sums of capital investment must be released into the Russian economy, from at home and abroad. Absent that, Russia's economic infrastructure will quite literally disintegrate as surely as the former Soviet fleet has been rusting away in port.

Challenges for Leaders

It is thus up to Russia's political leaders to devise a political, legal and administrative framework that can assure potential investors—Russian as well as foreign—that they can reasonably calculate the risks attendant upon a large-scale investment in Russia's future. If Russia fails in this fundamentally political task—whether under a democratic or authoritarian system—it can expect long-term economic stagnation at best and economic, social and political decomposition, and even disintegration, at worst. A comparison of international investment flows between Russia, on the one hand, and Hungary and China, on the other, is most revealing about the political and economic distance that Russia needs to travel in order to instill minimal investor confidence in its prospects. Between 1989 and 1996, according to the European Bank for Reconstruction and

Development (EBRD) opened in 1991 to help revive the economies of Eastern Europe, and the UN Economic Commission for Europe, Russia (with a population of just under 150 million) has attracted less than $6 billion in direct foreign investment, as compared with nearly $14 billion by Hungary (with a population of 10 million); China, by contrast, now receives about $40 billion in international investment *annually*. Comparing just Hungary and Russia, and converting investment and population ratios into a crude index of investor confidence, it is as if international investors had relatively 34 times more confidence in the investment prospects of Hungary than in those of Russia.

Obstacles to Doing Business in Russia

The magnitude of the task facing the Russian government is summed up in the *Fiscal Year 1998 Commercial Guide for Russia* published by the U.S. embassy in Moscow. Among the many roadblocks to doing business in Russia, the embassy mentions ownership disputes; high taxes and a frequently changing tax regime; lack of systematic and accessible credit information; corruption and commercial crime; the financial illiquidity of many Russian firms; changing requirements from regulatory agencies; lack of market information; an infant commercial legal framework; infrastructure problems (telecommunications, roads, banking systems, ports, etc.); payments arrears and frozen accounts; and frequent changes in government personnel. Post-Soviet Russia remains, according to the embassy report, "an extremely difficult country in which to do business."

Russia's current political system compounds this challenge in several ways: by affording Russia's licit and illicit economic clans privileged access to governmental resources, the winners of Russia's post-Soviet privatization process have been able to insulate themselves from popular resentment and, so far, from electoral revenge. Yet the extension of the vote to Russia's entire adult population gives the majority that has been excluded from Russia's post-Soviet transition the political possibility of challenging, or even reversing, those gains. Yergin and Gustafson note two main dangers within their positive scenario of the "Russian miracle": if the losers find their political voice or if the winners decide to protect their gains and themselves from popular scrutiny. But what if both are happening at the same time, as seems to be the case in Russia today? This would seem to be a prescription for political deadlock at best and a social explosion at worst, thereby underscoring the very different effects that take place when combining democratization and marketization in countries like Russia, as compared with combining a free market and democracy in stable Western systems.

Russia's heroic dissident writer Solzhenitsyn concurs. In a series of works dating back to the late 1960s, Solzhenitsyn has explained why he thinks it is not possible for Russia to make a rapid transition from a totalitarian Soviet system to a Western-type democratic one, even if that were desirable. In the deserted institutional and spiritual landscape of an eventual Soviet collapse, some kind of authoritarian order would be both necessary and desirable for Russia to have the chance to realize the promise of freedom for its peoples. Certainly, he understood what he called "the dangers and defects in authoritarian systems of government: the danger of dishonest authorities, upheld by violence, the danger of arbitrary decisions and the difficulty of correcting them, the danger of sliding into tyranny." But it was not authoritarianism that Solzhenitsyn found frightening but rather authoritarian regimes bound neither by tradition nor moral code, "which are answerable to no one and nothing." Solzhenitsyn concludes with a question that takes on added significance in light of Russia's painful movement past the Soviet period:

> *If Russia for centuries was used to living under autocratic systems and suffered total collapse under the democratic system which lasted eight months in 1917, perhaps—I am only asking, not making an assertion—perhaps we should recognize that the evolution of our country from one form of authoritarianism to another would be the most natural, the smoothest, the least pain-*

Reuters/Alexander Natruskin/Archive Photos

Russia, May 1994: Aleksandr Solzhenitsyn, born in 1918, was arrested while serving in the Red Army for criticizing Stalin. In 1970, the fearless novelist and exposer of the Soviet system won the Nobel Prize for Literature. He received the prize in Stockholm, Sweden, in 1974 while in exile in the West.

ful path of development for it to follow? It may be objected that neither the path ahead, nor still less the new system at the end of it, can be seen. <u>But for that matter we have never been shown any realistic path [of transition] from our present type to a democratic republic of the Western type.</u> And the first-mentioned transition seems more feasible in that it requires a smaller expenditure of energy by the people.

Just how much energy the Russian people have expended in trying to adapt to the combination of capitalism and democracy that is being attempted in the 1990s is reflected in Russia's ongoing demographic crisis, which is unprecedented in industrial societies at peace and not under epidemic assault. Key social statistics suggest that large sectors of Russian society are losing hope in the future.

Difficulties Are Greater for Russia

Under these circumstances, Russia cannot attain a stable liberal democracy *and* a mature market economy in any policy-relevant future. It is not that the values expressed in a liberal democracy are undesirable. Rather, the institutions required to sustain those values, which have evolved over the centuries and at enormous cost in lives and treasure in the Western world, cannot be built in the few short years implied by the concept of "transition" that is often applied to post-Soviet politics and economics. The difficulties of building a stable post-Soviet political and economic order are magnified in the Russian case, as compared with many East European states (for example, the Czech Republic) because (a) Russia's non-Communist civic institutions and traditions are among the weakest in the former-Communist world (the Russians having spent an extra generation under the Soviet system), and (b) Russia—due to its sheer size—is at a much further political-economic remove from Europe and the North Atlantic world. As a result, Western economic resources, to the extent that they are available, will have minimal effects in recasting the Russian economy and thereby helping to absorb some of the social and political shocks of the transition. To give just one example: according to the European Bank for Reconstruction and Development, foreign investment in Hungary between 1989 and 1995 amounted to more than 10 percent of the country's GDP; the same figure for Russia is less than one-half of one percent. Likewise, Russia has attracted only $47 per capita in direct foreign investment over the past six years, as compared with $326 by Poland, $585 by Chile and $130 by China.

Latin American Model

Based on the recent history of post-Soviet Russia, it is not the North Atlantic world that holds out a plausible model for Russia's political development but rather Latin America's experience with independence following the collapse of the Spanish Empire in the 1820s and extending through the latter part of the twentieth century. In Latin America then, as in Russia today, the collapse of imperial authority and the superimposition of liberal republican political constitutions had the effect of allowing entrenched economic elites to consolidate their hold on their countries' social, economic and political systems and exclude the mass of society from meaningful political participation indefinitely. Russia's post-1993, superpresidentialist constitution—in the absence of an effective presidential leader—has allowed Russia the practice of generally free and fair elections without the substance of meaningful popular or legislative influence on governmental policy. Fabulous wealth is being amassed at the same time that precious little investment in the country's productive assets or infrastructure is being made. Deputy prime minister for the economy Chubais, for example, managed to earn $278,000 between mid-April and mid-July 1996, when he worked for Yeltsin's presidential campaign. Meanwhile, Russia's wealthy keep the bulk of their assets abroad, where many keep residences "just in case." (Deputy National Security Adviser Vladimir Berezovsky himself took out Israeli citizenship in 1994 and obtained a forged U.S. green card, just in case.)

Little wonder that most Russians have few illusions that this state of affairs has much to do with political democracy. Under these conditions, Russia seems to be developing a hybrid Latin American-type political-economic system—a synthesis of the following:

- contemporary "Medellín" (drug trafficking) Colombia, with its parallel and interpenetrating criminal and civil states, which compete for resources and are to some extent interdependent with each other;

- mid-century Argentina under President Juan Perón, where the major industrial, agricultural and labor leaders were co-opted by the state, whose coffers were fueled by corruption and economic protectionism and which employed a mild xenophobia in order to rally the general populace behind the state; and

- twentieth-century Brazil, with its massive resource base and equally massive economic and social inequalities—indeed, the elite's access to such immense resources helps perpetuate its effective control of the system.

The combination of these three models appears to describe Russia's medium-term political development. Moreover, such a future is actually rather a good one, at least compared to Russia's horrific experience throughout the twentieth century, during which untold millions died at the hands of the Soviet Communist state. Such a scenario, however, is very far indeed from the examples of North Atlantic democracy that are implied when speaking about Russia's transitional politics. To the extent that this is so, it is important for the outside world to begin to realize that Russia's political and economic evolution and its relations with the rest of the world are two separate issues.

5

Implications for American Foreign Policy

THE PRECEDING ANALYSIS of Russia's political structure and functioning in the years since the collapse of the Soviet Union leads to the following conclusions about the Russian future:

First, it is most unlikely that Russia can become a liberal, market democracy on the North Atlantic model. Key preconditions for democratic development are absent: that is, the rule of law, a stable middle class, and a broad commitment to individualism, toleration, compromise and trust in civic affairs.

Second, even if this prediction proved wrong, Russia's path to political democracy would be prolonged and full of latent instabilities due to the effort to construct political democracy at the same time as a capitalist economic foundation is being attempted, and both without an adequate superstructure of reasonably functioning political institutions. Democratization is a very different process from the maintenance of an existing, proven democratic system.

Third, and as a consequence, for the forseeable future the primary political challenge for Russia is not the construction of democracy but the establishment of a minimally competent state, of whatever political coloration. The debility of Russia's post-Communist public institutions means that for Russia even to have a chance at the development of the rule of law, not to mention political democracy, building a strong (or competent) state is as important as the emergence of a vital civil society.

In this light, the challenge that Russia's political course presents for the United States is to begin distinguishing the issue of U.S. policy toward post-Soviet Russia from the problem of Russia's largely uncharted political evolution, democratic or otherwise. Russia's politics, and its political evolution, are currently in an especially fluid situation, as analysis of Russia's recent electoral history shows. Most of Russia's long-run futures are thus open. The unpredictability of Russia means that the West can ill afford to base its foreign policies on particular scenarios about the course of Russian politics. The international conduct of the Russian state, rather than the particular internal evolution of the regime, would better serve as the touchstone of Western policies toward post-Soviet Russia.

To date, the United States under the Bush and Clinton Administrations has chosen to focus on affecting Russia's long-term international behavior by seeking to help transform its domestic institutions in the short-term. In the process, the United States has avoided addressing Russia's current conduct at home and abroad where it has conflicted with international legal and political norms (such as in Chechnya, but elsewhere throughout the post-Soviet region as well), for fear of triggering a domestic reaction against the Yeltsin government, which they have seen as that country's best hope for democratic capitalism. The Group of 7 meeting in Moscow on April 19–20, 1996, illustrates the point: This summit of the United States and its key industrialized allies, scheduled two months before Russia's presidential elections, was clearly aimed at bolstering Yeltsin's chances at reelection. German Chancellor Helmut Kohl, when asked if the summit hadn't the effect of reinforcing Yeltsin's policies and political prospects, responded, "What's bad about that?" President Clinton himself compared the Russian war in Chechnya to the U.S. Civil War and implicitly compared Yeltsin to Abraham Lincoln as a way of marginalizing the issue in U.S.-Russian relations. Clinton did not contradict Yeltsin when the Russian president asserted, with the American President at his side, that there was no war going on in Chechnya.

A Middle Course

Critics of Administration policy have urged a contrary policy, one that confronts a Russia seen to have lost its wager on reform at home and bent on a kind of "neo-imperialism" abroad, at least in Russia's immediate vicinity (in Moldova, throughout the Caucasus and Central Asia). In fact, there is a middle course which is not indifferent to Russia's domestic prospects but which seeks to make its international relations the touchstone of American policy. This course, which could potentially integrate the perspectives of both the Administration and its critics, would seek to make Russia choose, on a case by case basis, between its parallel interests in seeking a dominant position (if not hegemony) in central Eurasia and integration into international institutions. The cause of international order in Eurasia, of Russian reform and even of the integrity of the Russian state itself requires that Russia and its neighbors observe restraint and mutual respect in their relations with each other and avoid commitments that will only have the effect of overburdening already weak economies and political systems. Given the weight and urgency of the problems, the United States and more broadly all the members of the North Atlantic Treaty Organization (NATO) would be well advised to focus their limited energies on the most important strategic and geopolitical issues involved in Russia's external relationships: ensuring the effective control of nuclear materials and weapons systems in Russia's unstable post-Soviet political, economic and social system; and encouraging a stable relationship between the two states whose interrelationship is critical for the security of post-Soviet Eastern Europe, i.e., Russia and Ukraine. (The fact that little analysis has been done on the effects that the expansion of NATO eastward would have on Russian-Ukrainian relations—as Russia would almost certainly seek to minimize Ukraine's existing security links with the NATO nations—calls into question the premise that expanding the alliance will improve rather than detract from European security.)

Compatibility of U.S. and Russian Interests

This is not to argue for some kind of confrontational policy toward Russia. The vital national interests of the United States and Russia are compatible with each other, as the historical sweep of Russian-American relations indicates. Indeed, Russia is the only major power with whom the United States has never had a shooting war (note the wars against England, 1775–83 and 1812–14; the undeclared naval war against France in the late 1790s; war against Spain, 1898; against Germany and Austria-Hungary, 1917–18; against Germany and Japan, 1941–45, and against Italy, 1941–43; and against China in Korea, 1950–53) suggesting that the cold war was an aberration rather than the norm in Russian-American relations. It is to suggest, however, that the contours of future U.S.-Russian relations should not hinge on whether or not Russia will become a democracy.

The Russian-American summit meeting held in Helsinki, Finland, on March 20–21, 1997, is instructive in this respect. Throughout the Clinton Administration, American diplomacy toward Russia has tended to focus on how best to transform Russia into a recognizable political democracy with a capitalist economic system. President Clinton's participation in the Moscow summit of the G-7 nations just two months before Russia's presidential elections in June 1996 underscored the degree to which Yeltsin personified that vision for U.S. policymakers. U.S. relations with Russia, in this view, will depend upon its transition toward a market democracy. What the Helsinki summit showed was that there remain important issues in Russian-American relations that cannot be subsumed under the con-

Presidents Clinton and Yeltsin held a wide-ranging summit meeting in Helsinki, Finland, in March 1997.

cept of Russia's democratic transition. This is so not only because that transition is necessarily a prolonged, unstable and contradictory process but also because Russia's very successes in democratization have legitimized some very hostile attitudes toward Western-style political democracy, market economics and even the United States, which is perceived by many in the Russian political elite as having given substantial partisan support to President Yeltsin in his internal policy disputes with the Russian opposition. (According to a spring 1997 poll conducted by the U.S. Information Agency, 59 percent of Russians believe that the United States is exploiting their country's current weakness in order to reduce it to a second-rate power.)

At Helsinki, Presidents Clinton and Yeltsin were able to negotiate an apparently impressive set of commitments in the fields of arms control, economic relations and on the thorny question of NATO expansion, which Yeltsin and the entire Russian political class have consistently stated they oppose. On close inspection, however, nearly every commitment undertaken by the two presidents depends upon the consent of the Russian Duma on a range of contentious issues, ranging from tax reform to oil-production policy to arms control and NATO, where the Russian legislature has long opposed Yeltsin's initiatives. For example, the U.S. proposal to move toward a third strategic nuclear arms reduction treaty (START III), in order to meet Russian technical and budgetary concerns over START II, comes into force only when the Duma ratifies START II, which it has so far refused to do because of separate policy objections to NATO expansion. Secondly, President Clinton's promise to provide incentives for U.S. businessmen to invest in Russia and to make it a peer of the G-7 economic council and the World Trade Organization, successor to the General Agreement on Tariffs and Trade launched in 1995, depend on the Duma passing liberalizing tax and investment legislation that it has so far vigorously resisted. Finally, it is doubtful that U.S. and NATO statements that there is "no foreseeable need" to deploy nuclear weapons and combat troops in new East European members of NATO will appease the Duma: this is a restatement of existing NATO policy and hinges entirely upon NATO's definition of its security requirements in Eastern Europe. Russia's democratically elected and representative parliament is thus likely to remain hostile on key issues in the Russian-American relationship and a complicating factor in that relationship for some time to come.

Weakness of Russian Duma

This does not mean that Russia's parliament can control the direction of Russian-American relations. Russian and American leaders are likely to resort to executive agreements that do not require legislative ratification instead of treaties where domestic resistance is deeply entrenched. Moreover, the actual policy influence of the Russian Duma is very weak under Russia's superpresidentialist constitution. But that is the point:

the easy assumption that many Americans make that electoral democracy abroad per se leads toward harmonious relations with the world's market democracies is called into question by the anti-market, anti-Western and even anti-U.S. sentiments that prevail among the majority in Russia's most democratically representative institution, i.e., its parliament, which contains a two-thirds majority of avowed Communists and chauvinistic nationalists. American interests in a stable relationship with post-Soviet Russia have in fact been advanced through a partnership with the most authoritarian element in the Russian political system, i.e., the Russian presidency.

Let this be clear: That Russia is not likely to become a democracy any time soon does not imply that Russian-American relations are fated to tension and collision (unless *Americans* insist that Russia become democratic as a precondition for normal relations). Writing in 1951, George Kennan gave serious thought to the foundations for a stable relationship between a future, post-Communist Russia and a democratic America. Kennan held three conditions to be essential for a healthy Russian-American relationship: that Russia renounce a messianic ideology, that it renounce totalitarianism and that it renounce empire. All three of these conditions now obtain. First, the intrusion of Communist ideology into Soviet foreign policy was renounced by Gorbachev by 1988 and by every Russian post-Soviet government since then. More-traditional ideas of national interest rather than of universal ideological missions—Communist or democratic—have taken root in Russian foreign policy consciousness. Second, Russia's chief political problem today is the establishment of a minimally competent state, one that can actually govern the land that it claims to rule. Even if Russia retains important elements of authoritarian government, the conditions for totalitarian rule in Russia have been broken. Third, the external relations of Russia have shown that, while it is very much interested in establishing diplomatic and geopolitical preeminence in the area described by the old U.S.S.R., it is not interested in the reacquisition of a formal empire. The economic costs (in terms of subsidy) and the political costs (in terms of the cohesion of Russia itself) of empire are widely recognized by Moscow as too high to pay. Moreover, as the Chechen war has shown, Russia may not even have the military capacity to obtain and then sustain empire. Indeed, in July 1997, Yeltsin signed a series of decrees that will bring about the most fundamental military reform in Russia's modern history. The military is to shrink by one third within three years.

The uses of military and economic force in the former-Soviet region by Russia since 1992 are more characteristic of the United States' historical conduct in Central America and the Caribbean than of an attempt to reconstruct a unitary political empire. Given the generally peripheral nature of U.S. interests in most of this region, there is no evident reason why Russian assertiveness toward neighboring states should trigger a collision in U.S.-Russian relations.

This does not mean that there will not be conflicts of interest between the two countries, as is normal in international politics: Russian-American differences over the expansion of NATO, the sale of nuclear reactors to Iran, the management of war and peace in the Balkans, and a score of major and minor issues of international politics and economics have already set in and will persist in relations between the two nations. These conflicts, however, have very little to do with Russia's democratic prospects. They have much more to do with traditional differences in national interests, as well as the profound weakness of the Russian state, the debility of Russia's public institutions and the still inchoate nature of Russian civil society. There is no reason to burden Russian-American relations with expectations that Russia can in a few years invent a democratic system which took centuries—and much turmoil, bloodshed, and heartbreak—to develop throughout the North Atlantic world.

Talking It Over
A Note for Students and Discussion Groups

This issue of the HEADLINE SERIES, like its predecessors, is published for every serious reader, specialized or not, who takes an interest in the subject. Many of our readers will be in classrooms, seminars or community discussion groups. Particularly with them in mind, we present below some discussion questions—suggested as a starting point only—and references for further reading.

Discussion Questions

What do you see as the prerequisites for the development of a democratic political system? What is the relationship between political institutions, economic systems, social structure and political culture in building and maintaining a stable democracy?

How does the Soviet historical legacy continue to shape the choices available to Russia as it charts its post-Communist path of political, economic and social development?

What are the challenges for Russia and other states in attempting to build both a capitalist economic system and a democratic electoral system at the same time?

Does the development of a heavily presidentialist political system help the creation of a new, post-Communist democratic state more than the establishment of a system which locates the preponderance of power in the legislative branch?

What are the necessary tasks that any government must perform? How effectively is the Russian government currently carrying them out, with what kinds of consequences for Russia's prospects for democracy?

Does Russia have a democratic future?

What difference would it make for the international interests of the United States if Russia failed to develop a democratic political system? Conversely, what problems might you identify in Russian-American relations even if Russia did develop a functioning political democracy?

Annotated Reading List

Goldman, Minton F., *Global Studies: Russia, the Eurasian Republics, and Central/Eastern Europe*. Guilford, CT, Dushkin Publishing, 1996. A survey of the post-Communist region that is appropriate for secondary-school education.

Handelman, Stephen, *Comrade Criminal: Russia's New Mafiya*. New Haven, CT, Yale University Press, 1995. A sobering portrait of Russia's emerging political-economic-criminal elites.

Hopf, Ted, "Russia and the U.S.: Growing Cooperation?" *Great Decisions 1997*, New York, Foreign Policy Association, 1997. An analysis of a set of issue areas in contemporary Russian-American relations.

Matlock, Jack F., Jr., "Dealing with a Russia in Turmoil." *Foreign Affairs*, May/June 1996. The former U.S. ambassador to Gorbachev's U.S.S.R. provides a policy framework for dealing with post-Soviet Russia.

Motyl, Alexander J., *Dilemmas of Independence: Ukraine after Totalitarianism*. New York, Council on Foreign Relations, 1993. A stimulating theoretical and empirical analysis of the many paradoxes of post-Communist political development, with particular reference to the problems facing Ukraine and Russia.

Nogee, Joseph L., and Mitchell, R. Judson, *Russian Politics: The Struggle for a*

New Order. Needham Heights, MA, Allyn and Bacon, 1997. An informative text summarizing and interpreting Russian politics since the collapse of the U.S.S.R.

Petro, Nicolai N., *The Rebirth of Russian Democracy*. Cambridge, MA, Harvard University Press, 1995. Argues that there exists an alternative Russian political tradition to absolutism and that this tradition is available to Russian leaders and society as they seek to constitute a stable post-Soviet political order.

Remnick, David, "Can Russia Change?" *Foreign Affairs*, January/February 1997. *The Washington Post's* Moscow correspondent from 1988 to 1991 provides a useful complement and at times contrast to the analysis put forward in this book.

White, Stephen, Rose, Richard, and McAllister, Ian, *How Russia Votes*. Chatham, NJ, Chatham House Publishers, 1997. A detailed analysis with many charts and opinion polls on Russian political attitudes and voting behavior between 1989 and the Russian presidential elections of 1996.

Yergin, Daniel, and Gustafson, Thane, *Russia 2010: And What It Means for the World*. New York, Random House, 1993. Provides five scenarios for Russia's political and economic future.

JUST PUBLISHED

Foreign Policy Forum

The Foreign Policy Association has just published the inaugural edition of **Foreign Policy Forum,** a collection of some of the most compelling speeches and articles by a variety of heads of state and policymakers.

This 168-page book provides readers with a "front row" seat at FPA's meetings and forums on topics ranging from trade and economics and our increasingly global community, to the United Nations and economic development. Each speech and article offers a glimpse into the personal perspectives and experiences of some of the world's most influential foreign policymakers and leaders.

Inaugural Edition

Foreign Policy Forum
$12.00; 168 pages
Published September 1997

The speakers featured in the **Foreign Policy Forum** addressed the Foreign Policy Association's members at events held in New York City. FPA holds meetings throughout the year, fulfilling one facet of its mission to serve as a catalyst for developing awareness, understanding of and informed opinion on U.S. foreign policy and global issues. To become a member of the Foreign Policy Association, please call the Membership Department at (212) 481-8100, ext. 238.

Includes speeches and articles by W. Bowman Cutter; William J. McDonough; Jeffrey E. Garten; James Gustav Speth; Bruce Stokes; Lester C. Thurow; and Linda Tsao Yang.